First Edition
Kane Miller, A Division of EDC Publishing

Compilation copyright © Jill Corcoran 2012
Illustrations copyright © J. Beth Jepson 2012

For information contact:
Kane Miller, A Division of EDC Publishing
PO Box 470663
Tulsa, OK 74147-0663
www.kanemiller.com
www.edcpub.com

Library of Congress Control Number: 2011904504

Manufactured by Regent Publishing Services, Hong Kong
Printed March 2012 in ShenZhen, Guangdong, China

ISBN: 978-1-61067-065-4

1 2 3 4 5 6 7 8 9 10

Dare to Dream...
Change the World

Edited by Jill Corcoran
Illustrated by J. Beth Jepson

Kane Miller
A DIVISION OF EDC PUBLISHING

Jill Corcoran's inspiration for *Dare to Dream … Change the World* came during a car ride, listening to NPR cover the uprising of the Egyptian people against their oppressive government. She has been to Egypt twice and remembers the extreme riches and poverty, as well as needing to be escorted by gunman with assault rifles to keep her safe. She was overcome by the courage of the Egyptian people and amazed by the role of social networking to bring their dreams and actions instantly to the rest of the world. To her, the tweets were like poetry, capturing the essence of the people's hopes, fears, strength and determination.

The title of this collection sprung into being during that car ride as well as the dream of a collection of poems by the best children's poets living today to share the spirit of dreaming + action = change and that each one of us can make the world just a little better.

www.daretodreamchangetheworld.com

Dare to Dream

By Jill Corcoran

Cocooned

Quiet

Dreams whisper

Crystalize

Grow, cell by cell

Thought by thought

Transforming

Transfixing

Larger and larger

Louder and louder

Pounding, kicking, wrestling,

Blooming

Bursting

To be free

To be.

The Child

By J. Patrick Lewis

Sylvia pushed into the wind,
Septembering the trees,
and hurdled over a railroad track
to a two-room shack
that never read "Browns Only."
It did not have to.

Under the billion-acre sky,
she wondered, *Did white girls
at 17th Street Elementary really
wear rainbow necklaces?*

Aunt Sally took her there once.
Eyes sharp as icepicks pierced
the windowpanes as if seeing
a Mexican for the first time.
Every door was locked with a
secret combination of frowns.

How can anyone ever get in?
Sylvia asked. *Someone must know
who has the right key…*

She looked up at her mother.
Maybe me.

Sylvia Mendez

In California in 1946, Hispanics were restricted to "Mexican schools." When ten-year-old Sylvia Mendez and her brothers were barred from a school for "Whites only," their parents filed suit to end separate education. The city of Westminster, California, claimed that fluency in English was the critical issue, but their case fell apart when eloquently bilingual Sylvia testified. The court ruled in the Mendez's favor, thereby paving the way for later civil rights victories. Today, Sylvia Mendez continues to fight and inspire others to stand up to discrimination and demand equal rights.

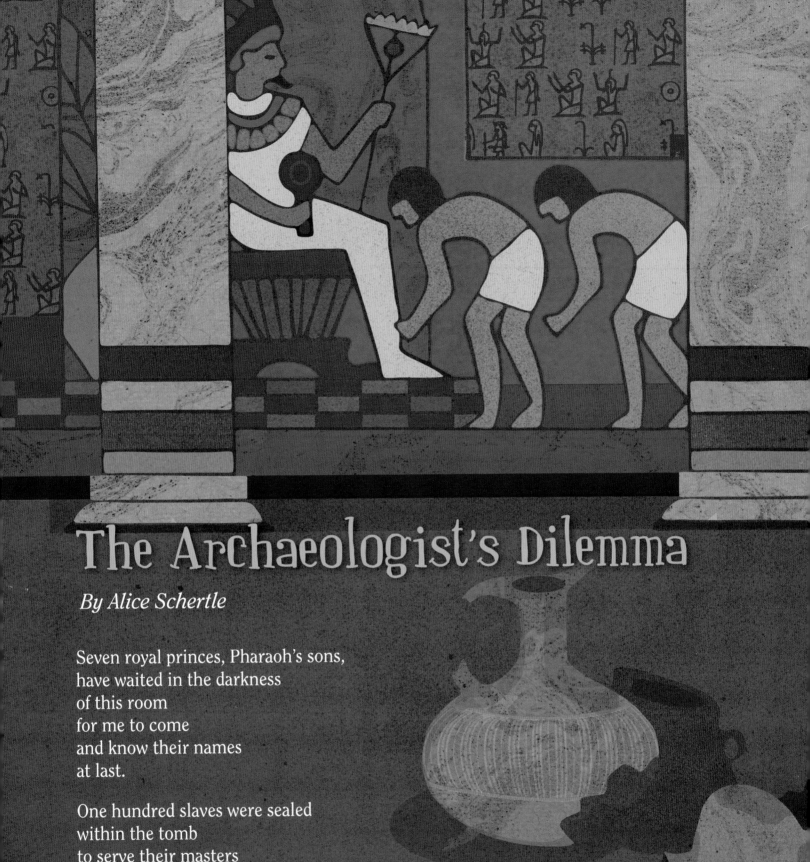

The Archaeologist's Dilemma

By Alice Schertle

Seven royal princes, Pharaoh's sons,
have waited in the darkness
of this room
for me to come
and know their names
at last.

One hundred slaves were sealed
within the tomb
to serve their masters
in the afterlife.

Forty spinning centuries have passed
and mixed the princely pieces
with the others.

Which are the bones of common men?
Which are the royal brothers?

Nicholas Cobb

By David L. Harrison

Four-year-old Nicholas Cobb
saw people living under
a bridge, asked
why.

Asking still as years passed,
Boy Scout Cobb decided to do…
something…
make a difference.
Fifty-four kids at City House
needed more than shelter.
They needed hope, a way to cope,
a gift of love,
a warm
coat.

That was something.

Nicholas asked friends to give,
left jars in barbershops,
made a website – Comfort and Joy,
did what he could
and
        money came in.

Ten years from the bridge,
Eagle Scout Cobb,
doing what he could,
bought fifty-four coats

By learning what it means
to ask not why
but how
to make
a difference.

Nicholas Cobb

As a young child, Nicholas Cobb saw a family living under a bridge. By the age of thirteen, he was calling on friends, family and businesses to help him raise money to buy coats for the homeless. In 2009, he raised $3,400. By 2010, he had founded the nonprofit Comfort and Joy, and raised $4,500 as his Eagle Scout project to buy coats for all fifty-four children living in a shelter in Plano, Texas. He invested the $10,000 he was awarded as an honoree in the 2010 National Make a Difference Day in Comfort and Joy. Nicholas continues to raise money through his website and continues to donate hundreds of coats as well as other necessities to those in need.

Under the Bridge

By Jane Yolen

Toll: money paid for upkeep of a bridge, or for the upkeep of the bridge owner by anyone who crosses from one side to the other.

Once trolls lived under the bridge,
so we thought, so we said,
nine feet tall and nine feet wide,
a hide like an alligator's.
Mean and green billy-goat eaters,
with grins as wide as a grave.
Who would want to save them?

Once hobos lived under the bridge,
dark and dangerous, so we said,
child stealers, drug dealers,
off-the-grid panhandlers,
man-handlers, living high on our taxes,
with mouths as mean as a miser's.
Who would want to help them?

But families under the bridge?
Far easier now to pay that toll.
Yet do not forget who we are—
also hobo, also troll.

G-Dog

By Joan Bransfield Graham

Homies
with shaved heads,
baggy grey pants
shuffle in.
It's Saturday morning
at the Probation Camp.
Fr. Greg Boyle–
G-Dog–
says a Mass, and,
when it's over,
hands out
his card.
"When you're
on the outs,
give me a call.
I'll find you
a job."
Founder of
Homeboy Industries
and Homegirl Café,
he'll also
kick you down
for some grub,
come up with clothes
for an interview,
listen.
Rival gangbangers
baking bread
together
because . . .
nothing
stops a bullet
like a
job.

Father Gregory Boyle

After service in Bolivia, Father Gregory Boyle, a Jesuit priest, was assigned to the poorest parish in Los Angeles, one with the highest concentration of gangs. He rode his bike around the "hood" and found "homies" whose "spirit is so sore, it hurts to be me." With respect, humor, and unconditional love, he searched for ways to help them change their world. Expanding a parish project, Jobs for a Future, he purchased an old bakery which became Homeboy Bakery, the "United Nations" of gangs, where enemies learned to work together. Affectionately known as "G-Dog" or "G," Father Greg has received numerous humanitarian awards, including the California Peace Prize, for his work helping thousands of former gang members find jobs and realize their ambitions.

By Some Stroke of Heaven

By Ellen Hopkins

Evil flourishes when good men do nothing.

Edmund Burke (paraphrased)

Long ago, when hominids roamed
wild in packs, like the wolves
whose voices made them tremble,
instinct fueled the need to gather summer
sustenance toward winter famine,
and the weak were culled, left
to the elements and predators.

Once, people existed in darkness
and when evil came howling,
they surrendered to its claim.

Humans, however, had capable brains.
They learned to capture fire, harness
its power, warm the hearths
inside their shelters. They knotted nets,
fabricated weapons, filled their larders.
But spears and arrows were double-edged
and survival belonged to the fittest.

Once, people dwelled in twilight,
and when evil came calling,
they hid behind their doors.

By some stroke of heaven, mankind
grew compassionate hearts, rich
with courage, and stashed within
them they found the will to scale impossible
peaks, sail impassable seas and forge
futures not free of obstacles
but brighter for conquering them.

Now, when people embrace a life
of light, should evil come chasing,
they hold their ground. Face it down.

This Moment

The Frank Family – Monday 7:30 a.m. July 6, 1942

By Georgia Heard

Stepping over puddles on Prinsengracht Street,
shoes soaked, heavy rucksacks on their backs,
coats, caps and scarves although it's warm July;
silence between them.
Anne wonders how others on the street
can act like it's a normal day;
no knots in their stomachs, no legs trembling with fear.
At her father's office building, a spice warehouse,
they open the door – sweet cinnamon fills the air.
Now it's quiet. Office workers haven't yet arrived.
They climb the narrow staircase to the small rooms
in the back of the secret annex

where this moment turns into days
into weeks and months
into two years hiding – waiting.
Eerily ordinary days –
Westertoren church clock chiming every half hour,
playing Monopoly with Peter,
cooking supper,
eating split-pea soup and potatoes with dumplings
washing up
listening to the radio at night for news of the war
like any family.

While in hiding Anne writes to *Kitty*.
Her words thread through
her dreams;
and later
ours –
thread through every moment –
ever after.

Anne Frank

On July 6, 1942, Anne Frank and her family went into hiding in an attic in Amsterdam. For the next two years, thirteen-year-old Anne kept a diary she addressed as "Dear Kitty."

In August, 1944, someone informed the Nazis, and Anne and her family were arrested and sent to concentration camps. Anne's father, Otto, was the only survivor. In 1947, *Anne Frank: The Diary of a Young Girl* was published. One of Anne's entries reflects her interminable hope, "In spite of everything I still believe people are basically good at heart."

Faith of a Mustard Seed

By Hope Anita Smith

In the attic, everything happens on a piece of paper: happiness, disappointment, fear,
Spite. I can laugh out loud. Shout. Make my voice heard. Tell
Of my love for a complicated boy.
Everything is documented.
I let my pen whisper my secrets into the ear of the page.
Still, I wish my dear Kitty could hear them first hand. I allow myself to
Believe that one day Peter and I will share a life together. That the
People we love will eat Shabbat dinner at our table. That we
Are only here until the world rights itself.
Basically, when someone soothes the beast.
Good always prevails. Doesn't it?
At least that's what I believe in my
Heart of hearts.

Jonas Salk Poem

By Elaine Magliaro

The word "polio" spawned an epidemic of fear.
Worried parents
Asked, "How is it spread?"
Wondered, "Will my child be stricken?"
Hoped someone would find a cure.

I would be a problem solver,
Find a way
To vanquish the unseen foe—
A virus crippling many.
I set to work in my laboratory.
Years passed into history.
Then time stood still
As I waited…waited to hear
The good news
That the vaccine I developed worked,
That it built a wall of immunity
Against the dread disease,
That it would protect the children—
Those who were most vulnerable.

President Eisenhower said he had no words to thank me.
I needed no thanks.
I had lived my dream to help mankind.
When asked who owned the patent on my vaccine, I replied,
"There is no patent. Could you patent the sun?"
It belonged to the people.

Jonas Salk

Jonas Salk once said, "It is always with excitement that I wake up in the morning wondering what my intuition will toss up to me, like gifts from the sea. I work with it and rely on it. It's my partner." Salk thought that the way nature worked seemed to be "quite magical." He entered medical school with the desire to become a medical researcher, to look for ways to prevent and find cures for diseases. In 1950, Salk was awarded a grant to fund research into polio. After five years, Salk and his team developed a vaccine that was declared safe and effective. At a special ceremony at the White House on April 22, 1955, President Dwight D. Eisenhower presented Jonas Salk with the U.S. Medal of Merit for his work.

My Polio Shot

By Janet S. Wong

The thought of a shot makes me sick.
I feel the prick in my arm over and over–
the pain growing larger–
even before it happens.
"This isn't going to be fun," I say.
My grandmother puts it another way:
she shows me her legs, one of them
slightly shorter and smaller than the other.
And she tells me about all the kids in her village
who died from polio, and those
whose legs shriveled up
like dried squash in the sun.

"You think it was fun," she asks,
"to stay in bed all year long, unable to walk,
acupuncture needles poked every day
into my swollen body?"
Grandmother pinches my arm
with a little shot of courage.

Jean-Michel Basquiat's boyhood song

By Curtis L. Crisler

I stepped on the cracks of sidewalks
not-scared-to-break-my-mama's-back,

not scared to know all time and space,
not scared to do what I must do, no matter

what daddy said. Life was the same ole
same ole, so I started painting my mind

on concrete New York sidewalks. I started
reading and reading, then reading more,

as if I would die if I couldn't capture words
in a peanut butter jar. I started spilling

my guts in crayon on New York buildings
'cause I didn't have the proper backyard

to play in. I accepted paint brushes as my
fingers and people as my toys and books

as real life 'cause the fire-spark in me blew
up like I had thrown up magical colors

that angels painted on rainbows. And
the music, the music that pumps its beat,

the music that thumps in my chest has
my brave heart looking to accept the rain,

the sun, the moon, to become the-king-
of-okay. I am okay—the joy-joy star.

Jean-Michel Basquiat

Jean-Michel Basquiat was a feverous outburst of passionate words and music on canvas. With classical music and hip hop beats flowing through his veins, he bloomed from low brow graffiti artist tagged SAMO, to the Radiant Child of a generation looking for hope. Basquiat died at the age of twenty-seven, yet in his short life he gained international rock-star status as one of the most important contemporary artists of his time and to this day continues to inspire artist, painters, muralists, and collagists. One of Jean-Michel Basquiat's most famous quotes is, "Since I was 17 I thought I might be a star."

word from the wise

By Denise Lewis Patrick

sooner, not later
you're gonna
step out
in the dark
to fight life on your own
same way
you stormed into this world
and
tore through
the years between then
and
now, but
you're a
true
warrior, child! already
full of dreams
we've never seen,
all
ready
to
shape and make them
real–you, who
has the sun
in your heart, will
ride
home
on light, yet
we know you can't stay:

the stars are calling you

the brilliant stars
are
calling
for
you

Gold

By Joyce Lee Wong

In scuffed brown
rented skates,
fastening my dreams
with knotted laces
triple looped above my ankles,
holding me tight as
my family's embrace

Olympic skater:
At seven, I saw myself there,
bright as my dragon necklace,
grandma's gift
shining gold.

At seventeen, skating Nagano:
My jumps ripple the air,
pulling time until it bends
like taffy–
folding upon itself
in overlapping lines
of caramelized grace.

Showered with flowers,
drenched in applause
I'm shaking with sobs
uncontrollable as laughter.
Through my tears,
like sun slanting through rain,
falling drops
sparkling tiny mirrors,
shines my truth:
I skated
my heart.

Around my neck,
Olympic silver,
gleaming circle,
lake
of tears.
Silver moon
luminous
reflecting
my dragon,
dream
glinting
gold.

Four years later I'm back,
skating the Salt Lake City Olympics.
I'm gliding,
sailing
smooth as a stone
skipped across water
then suddenly
falling–
quick as a scratched CD,
a hiccup in time
jarring as the knowledge
you're dreaming
startling you awake,
your dream elusive
as the last rays of afternoon sun.

Bronze medal
expansive as sunset–
rose shading orange
cloaked blue-black
night mourning light.

Michelle Kwan

The most decorated female ice skater in American history, California native Michelle Kwan holds silver and bronze Olympic medals, nine U.S. championships, and five world titles. In each competition, Michelle wore a Chinese good luck charm, a gold dragon necklace given to her by her grandmother. "A champion," Michelle says, "isn't someone who never loses or falls down. It's someone who gets back up. Someone who has heart." Michelle bounced back from disappointing silver and bronze medals at the 1998 and 2002 Winter Olympics to win her seventh U.S. women's figure skating title and her fifth world title in 2003. Her fifty-seven perfect scores are the most of any ice skater in history.

At 22, skating Nationals,
each spin lifting above ice
light as a hummingbird,
my balance delicate
as the iridescent curve
of a soap bubble
hovering in air.

Eternal spins
shaping space,
line of my limbs,
curve of my spine,
I am the vessel
on the wheel.

Imbibing icy breaths,
heady with flight,
my first place finish:
radiant
gold.

The Other Truth

By Jacqui Robbins

The truth is:
I can't shoot
Or dribble
Or jump.
I'm slow like cement
And honestly, I'm a little afraid of the ball,
Ever since second grade
When Jessica Z passed to me
And my nose didn't stop bleeding until after school.

But here I am:
On the bench
In the gym
Trying out
For the sixth grade team
And look who's here next to me: Jessica Z,
Who has grown since second grade,
And is built like a linebacker
So tall I could walk under her armpits.

She tells me:
Girl, you can't shoot
Or dribble
Or jump
And you're slow as dirt.
So really, girl, why are you here?
I don't think she means to be mean.
She just knows the truth
And isn't afraid of anything, least of all me.

So I tell her:
Because
I can see that basket stretch and swish,
Smell that rubbery bumpy ball,
Hear those squeaky sneakers on the court,
As good as you can.
Yes, I stink at basketball, but I never stop running,
And sometimes the ball goes in anyway,
And I work up a Gatorade-needing, eye-stinging sweat.

Besides, I add:
Just because I can't shoot
Or dribble
Or jump,
And I make syrup look speedy,
Doesn't mean I don't deserve to play. Girl.
And before Jessica Z can close her mouth, or kill me,
I hop off the bench,
And get my slow, smiling self to mid-court to strut my stuff.

The Greater Sum of Parts

By Julia Durango

The thing about Ashley Bryan
isn't that he is
painter and poet
storyteller and scholar
philosopher and veteran
brother and son;
nor is it
his collection of
songs and sea glass
driftwood and bones,
memories of love
dressed in
crepe paper flowers.

The thing about Ashley Bryan
is that
when he takes your hand
all those pieces come together
like a found art puppet
like cut-paper collage
like a thing called
grace.

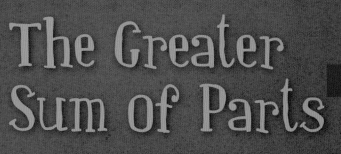

Ashley Bryan

Raised in a crowded Bronx apartment during the Great Depression, Ashley Bryan loved art from an early age. In his autobiography, *Words to My Life Song*, he recalls the crepe paper flowers his mother made to brighten the apartment, the colorful birds his father kept, and "learning to entertain himself" with art and music. He also remembers being turned down from a leading art institute at the age of sixteen, despite having the best portfolio because, "It would be a waste to give a scholarship to a colored person." But Ashley persevered and went on to become a graduate of Columbia University, a Fulbright Scholar, head of the art department at Dartmouth College, and one of today's most beloved, award-winning author/illustrators in the field of children's literature.

Grace

By Tracie Vaughn Zimmer

It's wiggling the hook out
of the fish's mouth
watching the flash and form
dissolve in dark waters.
It's bitter words swallowed
before they push past
the gates of angry lips.
It's a back turning
a head shaking
a refusal to hear
an ugly rumor,
a compromising joke,
lies.

It's sandbags
passed hand to hand
by a river
that's tipping over,
or a guest bedroom
bulging with refugees.
It's oatmeal
on cracked, swollen
fly-bitten lips.

A book
whose words
seem meant for the reader
or postcard scenery
sliding past a window.
It's the perfect silence
of an empty room
all one's own.

It's this hand,
reaching out to yours.

Temple Grandin

By Lisa Wheeler

Captures pictures with her mind
In a brain that's well-designed
To store every scene she sees
Like old movie memories

*"I think in pictures. Words are
like a second language to me."*

Didn't speak 'til she was four
Temper tantrums on the floor
Couldn't handle human touch
Crowds and noises were too much

*"You have got to keep autistic
children engaged with the world.
You cannot let them tune out."*

Teased and taunted as a kid
(No one saw things as she did)
Words were needed to explain
All the pictures in her brain

*"I can remember the frustration
of not being able to talk. I knew
what I wanted to say, but I could
not get the words out, so I would
just scream."*

Then when Temple was a teen
She invented a machine
That would hold her nice and snug
Like an artificial hug

*"The squeeze machine is not going to
cure anybody, but it may help them
relax; and a relaxed person will
usually have better behavior."*

Due to mom's determination
Temple got an education
Studied hard for each degree
'Til she earned her PhD!

*"I cannot emphasize enough the
importance of a good teacher."*

Now...

She employs imagination
Re-inventing cattle stations,
Solving problems in her brain
With designs much more humane.

*"I don't need a fancy graphics program
that can produce three-dimensional design
simulations. I can do it better and faster in
my head."*

Followed pictures in her head,
Opened doors where 'er they led
Visualized each stepping stone
Forged a pathway all her own

"I am different, not less."

The quotes used in the poem were taken from Temple's own writings.

Cussing at Cows

By Hope Vestergaard

I used to spring out of bed at dawn,
pull on coveralls and boots
and stumble to the barn
to feed the animals breakfast.
It was time alone with Dad,
if you didn't count the cows and pigs—
I didn't.
But that was before middle school,
where a whiff of barn
makes kids wrinkle their noses and whisper.
Now Dad leaves morning chores to me
since he says I'm so *capable*.
I slam the lids on the feed bins
and cuss at the nagging cows under my breath,
remembering that dumb thing
I said in history yesterday.
I toss hay bales into the feeder,
imagining I'm throwing them
at the gym teacher who mocks
my inability to do more than three pull-ups.
Heads up!
I carefully mix the mash for the pigs,
even though they squeal and complain ungratefully about the delay,
because I know they like it nice and wet.
As I wait for the water troughs to fill,
my bad mood drains away.
The rhythmic sound of munching cows and smacking pigs
is steady
and cozy
and comforting.

Temple Grandin

When she was very young, Temple Grandin was diagnosed with autism, a spectrum disorder few doctors had heard of when she was born. But Temple's mother was determined that she receive an education. She hired tutors and speech therapists, and read to her on a regular basis. (Temple eventually earned a PhD in Animal Science.) When she was a teen, Temple spent a summer at her aunt's cattle ranch in Arizona. There, she got the idea for her "squeeze machine" after seeing how the squeeze chute used to vaccinate cattle calmed them. She attributes much of her success on her ability to think in pictures.

Martha Graham Charts A Path

By Carol M. Tanzman

Papa said dance isn't proper.
    I would not listen.
Mama said sixteen's too old to start.
    I dare not listen.
The teacher said I am too short, too clumsy, too slow.
    I will not listen.

Instead, I listen to the music,
Rhythm drives my soul,
My body lunges, plunges across wooded floors–
Diagonal lines,
Unspoken signs,
Create form in space,
Meaning through time.

The fabric pulls, I wind and wrap it.
My partner spins, I cannot stop it.
The ways we move,
Apart–together–apart
Unveils the spirit, the trap, the graphing of my heart.

Martha Graham

Martha Graham began dancing at the relatively late age of sixteen, and never looked back. At age thirty-two, she established the Martha Graham Center of Contemporary Dance, creating a revolution in modern dance. Her choreography was defined and shaped by her movement technique of contraction from the center of the body, as well as her innovative use of fabric and social themes in her pieces. Graham was the first dancer to perform in the White House, and received the Presidential Medal of Freedom. She choreographed the final piece for her company when she was ninety-five. She wrote, "I have spent all my life with dance and being a dancer. It's permitting life to use you in a very intense way."

Dance

By Stephanie Hemphill

Dance
A percussive language of body
staccato of feet
arms that beat
air as breath and speech.
You can rhythm a Plains native.
You can quiet the lily abloom.
You can ignite the big boom
before silence.

Your movement will tell your story.
Swaddle your promises
like a cup of tears.
Come leap over what you fear.

Dance beyond the ocean's lip,
Do not be confined by the moon.
Let your movement lead you.

Painter

By Lee Bennett Hopkins

*"Where I was born and where and how I lived
is unimportant. It is what I have done with
where I have been that should be of interest."*
– Georgia O'Keeffe.

Sky will always be.
So shall I.

Feel my sudden thrill
as I stand atop
a beloved red hill.

Hear my silent voice rush
from charcoal, paint, a well-used brush
as I speak with hues –
vibrant violet, a grandeur of green –
bringing to life what I have seen.

Sense my strength
of a gigantic flower,
dry, desolate desert sands
I hard-studied hour after patient hour.

View my
ancient skulls of deer,
horse,
dried up ram –

then you'll know just who I am.

Yes.

Sky will always be.
So shall I.

So shall I.

Georgia O'Keeffe

"I have but one desire as a painter – that is to paint what I see, as I see it, in my own way…"
– Georgia O'Keeffe

Georgia Totto O'Keeffe was born near Sun Prairie, Wisconsin. At a time when work by women artists went unrecognized, she distinguished herself as one of America's most important innovative artists as early as the 1920s. Due to her passion for New Mexico, she left New York society to live there and paint until her death at the age of ninety-eight. The Georgia O'Keeffe Museum opened in 1997. It is the only museum in the world dedicated to an internationally known American woman artist.

Cloudscape

By Rebecca Kai Dotlich

I found a journal from sky once.
One page was titled:
Cursive in Prussian blue.
It was filled with scripts of air,
a wash of watercolor,
a flake-white calla lily,
talk of blooms and blossoms
fit for a museum; so gallant,
so lovely a brushwork of
space on canvas; sky said:
"Life, meet art." And,
"Art, meet life."
In the center of a day,
each day, are lines upon a canvas,
an abstract image that floats
like a spirit somewhere
down around the heart
and out from fingertips.
Sky told me so.

Journal of 73 Seconds

By Joyce Sidman

This is it.
We are set.
Locked, strapped, velcroed in tight.
Switches flipped, buttons pushed.
Lights blinking in glorious harmony.

So much packed in this tiny cockpit.
So much prep, so much hope.
So many hearts riding within our hearts.

Countdown begins.
Am I afraid? A tiny part of me,
behind all the thrill.
I'm keeping that fear in my back pocket,
like an extra lesson plan.
Never know when I might need it.

Rumbling erupts,
barrels toward us like the thunder
of ten thousand fireworks:
louder, *louder, LOUDER*

and slowly,
        slowly,
we lift, shaking and shuddering.
The Earth tries to hold us back,
but we stagger upward,
bounced and buffeted,
every moment more certain,
every second more free.

Pressed to my seat,
I feel suddenly solo ...
me, Christa,
        or not even Christa anymore,
just a spark of being
piercing the sky,
tingling with joy;
feeling, to the ends
of my fingertips, that even
if I went no further,
this moment
        would be enough–

Christa McAuliffe

As part of NASA's plan to put an "ordinary citizen" in space, high school history teacher Christa McAuliffe was chosen from 1,100 applicants to undergo the rigorous training necessary to accompany the crew of the Challenger space shuttle in January, 1986. Christa planned to broadcast "space lessons" on the shuttle's closed circuit TV for school children back on Earth, so that they could better understand space travel. She also planned to keep a journal, "an ordinary person's diary," she said, "just as the earlier American pioneers did when they traveled west." Tragically, the Challenger exploded in midair only seventy-three seconds after lift-off, killing all seven people aboard. Although she was thrilled to take part in a space voyage, Christa felt her most important work was in the classroom, saying, "I touch the future. I teach."

And Then There's Air

By Marilyn Singer

There's water, earth—and then there's air.

Each bat or bird or butterfly

so easily winging overhead

makes us long to know the sky.

Flying's always in our dreams,

in books and paintings, songs, cartoons.

We yearn to travel through the clouds.

We try with rockets, planes, balloons,

with flying carpets, broomsticks, kites,

with superpowers we invent

to go where no one's gone before

(or simply where those pigeons went).

Alien

By Rose Horowitz

In the dark, he was the town's king
of all action, motion and light.
He was the boy who could sing
behind the camera and show his fright.

He made movies starring
his sisters when he was eleven.
As a teen, he hung at Universal, bearing
his desire to film. Heaven

hit when some studio execs
took notice. His first big hit was *Jaws*,
its shark terrifying, full of complex
effects, he was now a great success.

But the fantasy of *E.T.* and *Close Encounters*
were one thing. Older, he changed tone
and filmed *Schindler's List* in black and white,
the story of a German who

saved hundreds of Jews from the camps.
Wise, he had big plans and set
out to record the voices of thousands of champs,
preserving for children the survivors' tales, he let

history live. This was the man, once a boy,
who played with toy trains and made his choice.
He crashed them to create special effects,
movies became his voice.

Steven Spielberg

Steven Spielberg hated school and often felt like an outsider, but as a young teen he became a local celebrity, making and showing movies starring his sisters and friends. After his family moved to California, he started to hang out at the lot at Universal Studios and would wear a suit and carry a briefcase to look like he was going to work so he could get through the gate. And at twenty-one, he was hired as a television producer. Starting with *Jaws* in 1975, many of Spielberg's films were major box office hits. He won the American Academy Award in 1994 for Best Director for *Schindler's List*, and in 1998, for *Saving Private Ryan*.

Projecting Greatness

By Alan Katz

It will take more than two days to watch
every movie Steven Spielberg's ever made.
During those 48+ hours, you'll face aliens.
Vicious sharks.
Fierce dinosaurs.
The harsh casualties of war
and uncertainties beyond comprehension.
You'll laugh.
Cry.
Gasp.
Swim for your life.
Run for your life
and have the time of your life.
You'll soar to new heights.
Yet plunge to new depths.
You will be filled with anger.
Fear.
Surprise
And wonder.
And when you get up out of the darkness
you'll step into a whole new light
and suddenly believe in the power of…
everything.
Then…
I'm pretty sure you'll want to phone home about it.

Just Like That

By Laura Purdie Salas

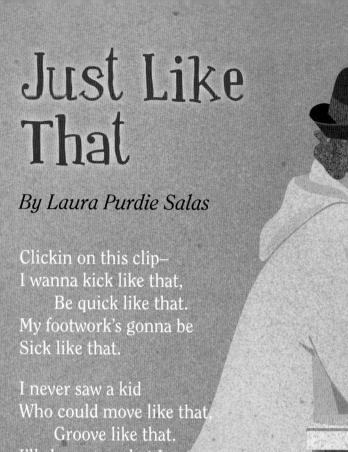

Clickin on this clip–
I wanna kick like that,
      Be quick like that.
My footwork's gonna be
Sick like that.

I never saw a kid
Who could move like that,
      Groove like that.
I'll show you what I got
I'm gonna prove like that.

All around the world
We watch the screen like that.

From Omaha to Seoul
And in between like that.

We're just a link away–
What's it mean like that?

I can see myself tomorrow
In a scene like that.

I can dream like that.

I can dream like that!

Chad Hurley, Steve Chen and Jawed Karim

Chad Hurley, Steve Chen and Jawed Karim co-founded YouTube in 2005, creating a simple user interface for easily sharing videos and responses online. The three young men met while they were all working for PayPal, an e-commerce company. They eventually decided to strike out with a business of their own. Finance and technology experts were skeptical about their idea for YouTube, but the YouTube founders disregarded the naysayers and pressed ahead – eventually changing not only their own lives, but those of millions of people around the globe. Jawed says that his favorite YouTube videos "illustrate what YouTube is all about, namely that anyone who has a good idea can just take that idea and make it happen."

A Place to Share

By Kelly Ramsdell Fineman

You could say they took something hard
    and made it easy.
You could say they reached out to the wide world
    and made it smaller.
You could say they shared their skills
    so others could share their talents.
You could say they created a real community
    within a virtual space.
You could call it a triumph of technology,
    a credit to creative thinking,
    an energized innovation.
Or you could call it YouTube.

Ripples

By Bruce Coville

No one acts in isolation
And no act leaves the world the same.
Words and gestures ripple outward,
What shores they reach we cannot name.

All our lives end in a riddle –
A mystery without an answer,
For even gone we ripple on,
Like a dance without the dancer.

Did you extend a friendly hand?
Did you lift a battered spirit?
The one you helped helped someone else
Ah! Now we're getting near it.

That second someone dropped despair
Did not give in, instead revived
To teach, to love, to fight, to dare,
And what you've done lived on, survived.

On and out the circle widens,
Past all hope of comprehending.
The slightest touch can change the world
Healing, helping, lifting, mending.

Actions last for generations
Our fathers' mothers mold our hearts.
We in turn shape all that follows;
Each time we act, a ripple starts.

Poets

Jill Corcoran

Jill Corcoran has marketed everything from sneakers to cereal and created her own company, LAUNCH! New Product Marketing, to help make many dreamers' dreams come true. Now a literary agent and poet, Jill continues to work with dreamers. Jill's poem "Pirates" was published in Lee Bennett Hopkins' *I Am the Book*. She lives with her husband, three kids, two labs, two cats and two guinea pigs in Los Angeles, CA.

www.jillcorcoran.com
www.daretodreamchangetheworld.com

J. Patrick Lewis

A professional skateboarder, martial artist, crocodile wrestler and opera singer, J. Patrick Lewis also writes children's picture/poetry books, over seventy-five of them to date. He has visited 475 elementary schools around the world. Recently, he received the 2011 NCTE Award for Excellence in Poetry for Children, and is the Poetry Foundation's U.S. Children's Poet Laureate (2011-2013).

www.jpatricklewis.com

Alice Schertle

Alice Schertle is a hermit who lives somewhere in the woods of Massachusetts. When she is not collecting owl pellets or poking mushrooms with a stick she likes to write poems and picture books. Her poetry has won many awards including the Lee Bennett Hopkins Award for *Button Up! Wrinkled Rhymes*, honored as the best children's poetry book of the year. She was last seen following bear tracks around a boulder.

David L. Harrison

David L. Harrison grew up in Missouri where he spent his days crawling through caves, catching snakes, the usual stuff. He could pitch baseball and play trombone, but not at the same time. In college, his English professor urged him to take up writing. After graduate school, he did. Eighty books later, he's still at it and still loving it.

www.davidlharrison.com

Jane Yolen

Jane Yolen is often called "the Hans Christian Andersen of America," because of the many fairytale stories and poems she has written. She is the author of over 300 books. That number makes some people gasp, but she shrugs and says, "I just write them one at a time, and boy, do I love writing!" She lives winters in an old Victorian farmhouse in Massachusetts and spends her summers in Scotland.

www.janeyolen.com

Joan Bransfield Graham

Award-winning author/poet Joan Bransfield Graham (*Splish Splash, Flicker Flash*) grew up on a barrier island along the southern coast of New Jersey, wondered what was on the other side of the ocean, and found out. As a child she wrote to pen pals in Japan and Holland. Now, an avid photographer, she enjoys exploring the world – including an author visit to Morocco. She loves encouraging children to use their imagination and think creatively.

www.joangraham.com
www.childrensauthorsnetwork.com/author/JBG.htm

Ellen Hopkins

Ellen Hopkins, "the bestselling living poet in America," is the author of twenty nonfiction children's books, eight *New York Times* bestselling young adult novels and the first of many adult verse novels. Ellen vows to keep writing for both teens and adults "until they have to pry my cold, dead fingers from the keyboard." Ellen lives near Carson City, Nevada, with her husband, son, two dogs, one cat and two ponds (not pounds) of koi.

www.ellenhopkins.com

Georgia Heard

Georgia Heard finds poems wherever she goes: watching orangutans in the jungles of Borneo; speeding down the Great Wall of China in a luge; and at home-sweet-home where she lives near the Atlantic Ocean with her husband, son and dog. She teaches poetry workshops across the U.S. and in Canada, Asia, the Middle East, South America and Europe. Her newest poetry collection is called *The Arrow Finds Its Mark: A Book of Found Poems*.

www.georgiaheard.com

Hope Anita Smith

Hope Anita Smith is the author of *The Way A Door Closes, Keeping the Night Watch* and *Mother Poems*, which she wrote and illustrated. Hope is a choreographer. She creates routines for words that allow them to dance across the page. Hope conducts writing workshops for all ages and is a motivational speaker. She resides in Beverly Hills, California.

www.hopeanitasmith.com

Elaine Magliaro

Elaine Magliaro is a published poet who has worked with kids and words most of her life, first as a teacher for thirty years and then as a school librarian for three. She also taught a children's literature course at Boston University for seven years. Sometimes she inspired her students to write poems – more often they inspired her!

www.wildrosereader.blogspot.com

Janet S. Wong

Janet S. Wong is the award-winning author of twenty-four books for children. A frequent speaker at schools, libraries and conferences, Wong has performed at the White House and has been featured on *CNN, Fine Living's Radical Sabbatical*, and *The Oprah Winfrey Show*. Her most recent books are ebooks: *Once Upon A Tiger: New Beginnings for Endangered Animals* and the *PoetryTagTime* anthologies.

www.janetwong.com

Curtis L. Crisler

Curtis L. Crisler learned to use his imagination from comic books, daydreaming in class, and learning about the people around him. He loves writing about the worlds of characters he creates in the merry-go-round inside his head. Published in books and magazines, Crisler's poetry has been adapted to theatrical productions in New York and Chicago.

www.poetboyworks.com

Denise Lewis Patrick

Denise Lewis Patrick, a Louisiana native transplanted to New Jersey, has written everything from poetry to puzzles to exhibit text for Cincinnati's Underground Railroad Museum. When she was a girl she loved cooking with her dad, climbing trees, and reading. These days, she still loves cooking and reading. She's the author of many books, including three featuring *American Girl* historical character, Cécile Rey. Sadly, her four sons have insisted that she retire from climbing trees.

www.deniselewispatrick.com

Joyce Lee Wong

Joyce Lee Wong is the author of *Seeing Emily*, a verse novel chosen as one of The New York Public Library's Books for the Teen Age 2007, in which Joyce weaves her love of painting into her story and poems. A lawyer and teacher, Joyce lives with her family in Los Angeles, where she wields both pen and paintbrush every moment she can.

www.joyceleewong.com

Jacqui Robbins

Jacqui Robbins is a writer, teacher, parent, director, soup-lover and baseball fan from Michigan. You might have found her first book *The New Girl…And Me* in your box of Cheerios – it was featured in over 1,000,000 of them. Her second book, *Two of a Kind*, was released in 2009 to rave reviews. She still can't dribble.

www.jacquirobbins.com

Julia Durango

Julia Durango lives in an old house by the Illinois River where she likes to daydream, write stories, root for underdogs, and believe in heroes. Some of her favorite things include: her boys, her dog, Doctor Who, cherry trees, Zelda, salsa music, Mexican food, snow days, and a tall stack of books on the nightstand.

www.juliadurango.com

Tracie Vaughn Zimmer

Tracie Vaughn Zimmer loves to read, write and teach poetry, which she does in the same school where she once attended long, long ago, back when cell phones didn't yet exist. She lives in southern Ohio with two dogs (one naughty, one nice) two kids (messy, but charming), four turtles (quite shy, truth be told), and a cat with a spare paw.

www.tracievaughnzimmer.com

Lisa Wheeler

Lisa Wheeler has had many jobs, most of them involving bad smells. "I've washed diapers, scrubbed toilets, and even spent a few months as the best night-crawler wrangler on a small island." But her favorite job, hands-down, is writing. "Fresh books are one of my favorite smells – bonus!" With over thirty in print, Wheeler plans to keep her nose in the books.

www.lisawheelerbooks.com

Hope Vestergaard

Growing up with eleven siblings, Hope Vestergaard developed observation skills and a sense of justice that help her write funny, honest books for children. Hope's first published poem was written at age seven: "When I was little, I ate a light bulb and it tasted good." It wasn't a metaphor. Hope lives on a Michigan farm with pigs, horses, and cows. She rarely cusses at them.

www.hopevestergaard.com

Carol M. Tanzman

Carol M. Tanzman was a dancing poppy in a production of *The Wizard of Oz* that toured to Moscow, an abstract chicken in a Massachusetts mime company, and the assistant director for a play in Germany where her major responsibility was making sure the sheep entered and exited on cue. She's the author of the YA contemporary thrillers *dancergirl* and *Circle of Silence*.

www.caroltanzman.com

Stephanie Hemphill

Stephanie Hemphill has been a teacher's aide, an accountant, an office manager, a waitress, a retail clerk and a nanny, among other jobs. She loves being an author. She has written several award-winning books, including *Your Own, Sylvia: A Verse Portrait of Sylvia Plath*, which received a Michael

J. Printz Honor. Her latest novel in verse, *Sisters of Glass*, is set in the Renaissance. Stephanie lives in Chicago, but writes everywhere.

Lee Bennett Hopkins

Lee Bennett Hopkins, a celebrated poet, is the recipient of the NCTE Award for Excellence in Poetry for Children and a Christopher Award for his autobiographical *Been to Yesterdays: Poems of a Life*. Lee holds the Guinness World Record for most prolific anthologist of poetry for children – 113 books and counting!

www.leebennetthopkins.com

Rebecca Kai Dotlich

Rebecca Kai Dotlich grew up in the Midwest building snowmen, exploring trails, reading comic books and waiting on the ice cream man. She gives poetry workshops and visits classrooms across the country. Her poetry appears in anthologies and textbooks, and has been featured on *Reading Rainbow*. She still enjoys building snowmen and waiting on the ice cream truck.

www.rebeccakaidotlich.com

Joyce Sidman

Joyce Sidman is the author of many innovative poetry books, including the Newbery Honor-winning *Dark Emperor & Other Poems of the Night*. Her book *This Is Just To Say: Poems of Apology and Forgiveness*, has been adapted as a school play. She teaches poetry writing in her home state of Minnesota, and attempts to keep up with her squirrel-obsessed dog on daily woodland hikes.

www.joycesidman.com.

Marilyn Singer

Marilyn Singer wrote her first poem in first grade. Since then, she has published over ninety books in many genres – but she likes writing poetry the most. Her books include *A Stick Is an Excellent Thing* and the award-winning *Mirror Mirror: A Book of Reversible Verse*, for which she created the "reverso" form. An avid ballroom and swing dancer, Marilyn lives in Brooklyn, NY and Washington, CT with her husband (and favorite dance partner) plus several pets.

www.marilynsinger.net

Rose Horowitz

Rose Horowitz is a poet and award-winning journalist. She has been published in *The New York Times, Forbes, The Los Angeles Times* and many other publications. Rose remembers going to see *Jaws* in Queens, NY during the summer of 1975 and being terrified while sitting at the movies on her first date.

Alan Katz

Alan Katz is a funny, funny man with work ranging from *Take Me Out of the Bathtub and Other Silly Dilly Songs,* to *Poems I Wrote When No One Was Looking.* A six-time Emmy-nominated TV writer for *The Rosie O'Donnell Show,* many animated shows, the Grammy Awards and Tony Awards, Alan has created comic books, trading card sets, web videos, TV commercials and hundreds of other special projects for kids and their parents.

www.alankatzbooks.com

Kelly Ramsdell Fineman

Kelly Ramsdell Fineman is an award-winning poet whose work for children has appeared in *Highlights for Children* magazine and in books for the commercial and educational markets, including her recent picture book, *At the Boardwalk.* Although she can be found many places on the internet, she has not posted anything on YouTube – yet.

www.kellyfineman.com

Laura Purdie Salas

Laura Purdie Salas is the author of *Bookspeak! Poems About Books* and *Stampede! Poems to Celebrate the Wild Side of School* plus more than 100 other books for kids and teens. She loves to write all sorts of things, but poetry is her favorite! She does not spend all day watching YouTube videos. Really.

www.laurasalas.com

Bruce Coville

Bruce Coville has been a teacher, a toymaker, a magazine editor, a gravedigger and a cookware salesman. He has written 100 books for children and young adults, including *My Teacher Is an Alien.* He lives in an old brick house in Syracuse, NY, with his wife, illustrator Katherine Coville, and three cats who remain supremely unimpressed with his accomplishments.

www.brucecoville.com

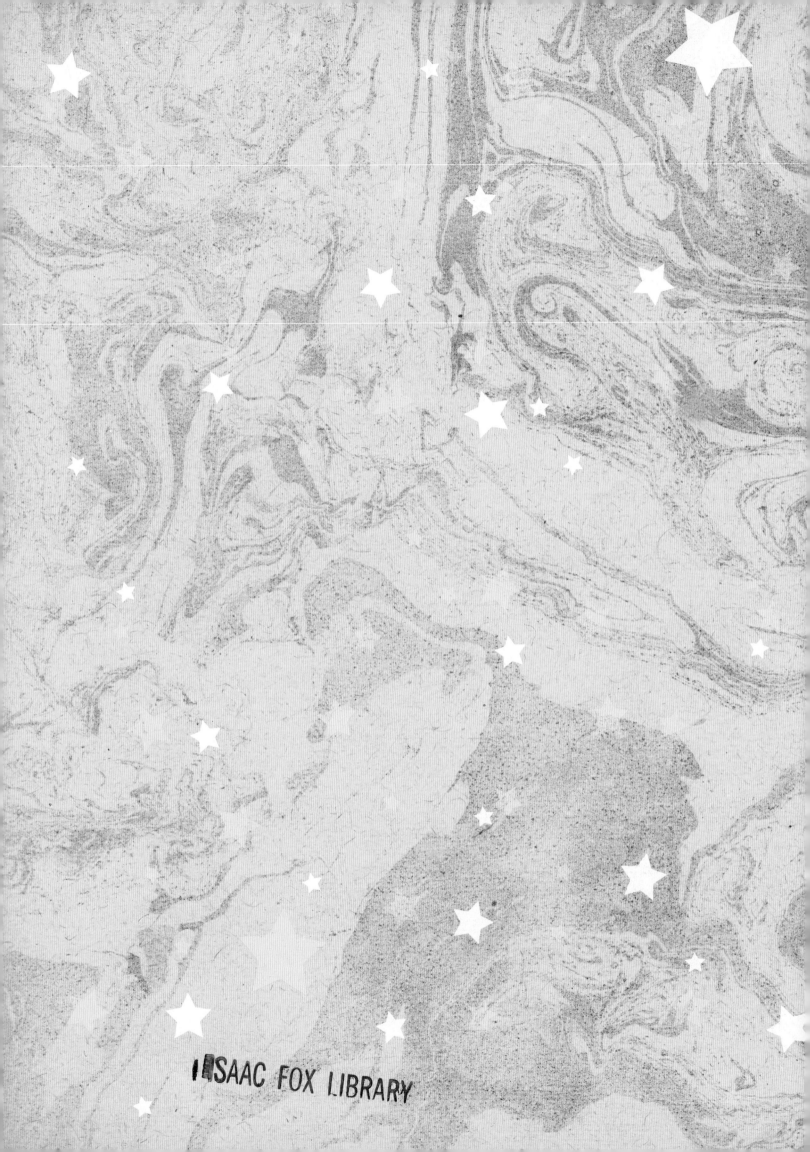